Coco Coping

Copyright @ 2026 by Lattishia Smith-Harvey

ISBN: 979-8-9891568-9-4
Independently published by
Lattishia Smith-Harvey and Janiya Stewart

All rights reserved. No part of this book may be reproduced,
stored in a retrieval system, or transmitted in any form or by any
means, electronic, mechanical, photocopying, recording, or
otherwise, without prior written permission from the publisher

ANXIETY

I0167769

My Best Baby Ever

To my sweet Milani,

From the very moment you arrived,
you filled my world with joy, laughter,
and a love deeper than I ever imagined.
You are my first grandbaby, my sunshine,
my tiny best friend, and my 'best baby ever.'

Watching you grow, explore, and sparkle
through life has been one of my greatest blessings.
You call me 'Grandma,' but the truth is…
I learn from you every day—how to
love brighter, dream bigger, and see
the world with wonder.

This book is for you, my precious girl.
Because you inspired it.
Because you deserve stories filled with magic
and comfort. Because you are a gift
God hand-picked just for me.

I adore you, Milani—
today, tomorrow and always.

My heart is forever yours.

Love, Grandma
(Lattishia Smith-Harvey)

Milani & Her Best Baby Ever

A Dreamling Guide to Big Sister Love

Once upon a time, there was a little girl named Milani, but everyone who loved her most called her M&M. M&M is three years old, curious, playful, and full of sparkle. One day, Mommy smiled a special smile and placed M&M's tiny hand on her belly. "There's a baby growing in here," Mommy said softly. M&M's eyes got wide. "A baby?" she asked. Yes," Mommy said. "You're going to be a big sister."

As the months went by, M&M learned
all about babies.
She helped Mommy rub her belly.
She talked to the baby inside.
She practiced saying, "Hi, baby sister."
Daddy told her,
"Being a big sister means you get to
love in a brand-new way."
M&M liked that... most days.

Then one day, the baby came.
Her name was Araya, but Grandma
called her Ry Ry.
Everyone smiled at Ry Ry.
Everyone held Ry Ry.
Everyone said, "Look at the baby!"
M&M loved her baby sister...
but her heart felt funny.

M&M loved baby Ry Ry so much that she wanted to keep her safe. Sometimes, when other kids wanted to hold Ry Ry, M&M would cross her arms and say, "No, that's my baby sister!" She felt like a little protector.

But other times, when no one was looking, M&M would pop a pacifier in her own mouth or curl up and cry, missing the days when she was the littlest one.

HAPPY.

PROUD.

LEFT OUT.

CALM
(Belly Breathing)

Sometimes M&M felt happy.
Sometimes she felt proud
and sometimes...
she felt left out.
Mommy was busy.
Daddy was busy.
M&M thought,
"Am I still the baby?"
Her chest felt tight.
Her eyes felt watery.

When M&M went to Grandma's house,
everything felt different.

Grandma scooped her up and said,
"There's my best baby ever!" M&M giggled.

Grandma rocked her
to sleep, brushed her hair, and
whispered,
"You can be a big sister and
Grandma's baby too.

M&M smiled and said,
"Grandma... you're my best baby ever."

One day at Grandma's house, M&M felt so many feelings all at once. She didn't know whether to cry, hide, or just be a baby again. Grandma noticed and gave her a warm hug.

"Let's take a deep belly breath together," Grandma said. "I have a special friend to help us."

She brought out a cuddly Dreamling, all soft and orange with fluffy pink hair and a little blanket.

"This is your Belly-Breath Dreamling," Grandma said. "Let's practice together."

She put the Dreamling on M&M's tummy. As M&M breathed in, the Dreamling rose up. As she breathed out, it gently fell. She did this a few times until M&M felt calmer.

M&M practiced her belly breathing.

Grandma said, "It's okay to have big feelings. When you feel overwhelmed, you can always come to me or cuddle your Dreamling. We can breathe together and find your calm place."

And just like that, M&M knew she had a way to feel safe and loved, whether she was a big sister or Grandma's "best baby ever."

Grandma taught M&M some special things to help her big feelings:

Name the feeling

"When your heart feels heavy," Grandma said, "you can say, 'I feel sad'."

Special time alone

Every visit, Grandma and M&M had their time just the two of them.

Play with baby

Sometimes M&M played baby with her dolls. Sometimes Grandma rocked her too.

M&M learned something very special:

Love doesn't get smaller.
It gets bigger.

Mommy loved the baby.
Daddy loved the baby.

And they still loved M&M just as much as always.

And no matter what,
to Grandma,
M&M would always be...
The Best Baby Ever.

Belly Breathe Guide

Built-In Coping Skills
Parents and Kids

These are already woven into the story,
but here's what it teaches gently:

- Naming feelings ("I feel sad / left out")

- One-on-one special time

- Reassurance that regression is normal

- Deep breathing for big emotions

- Feeling important with "helper" roles

- Permission to still be a baby sometimes

Check out these other books presented by the author:

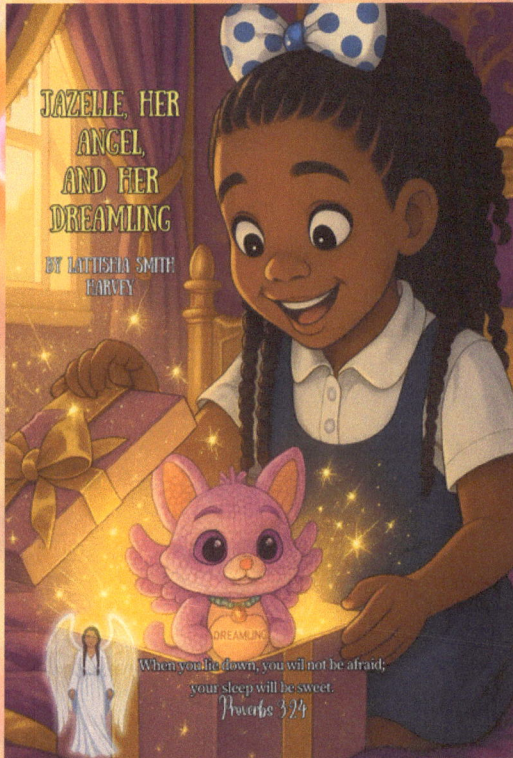

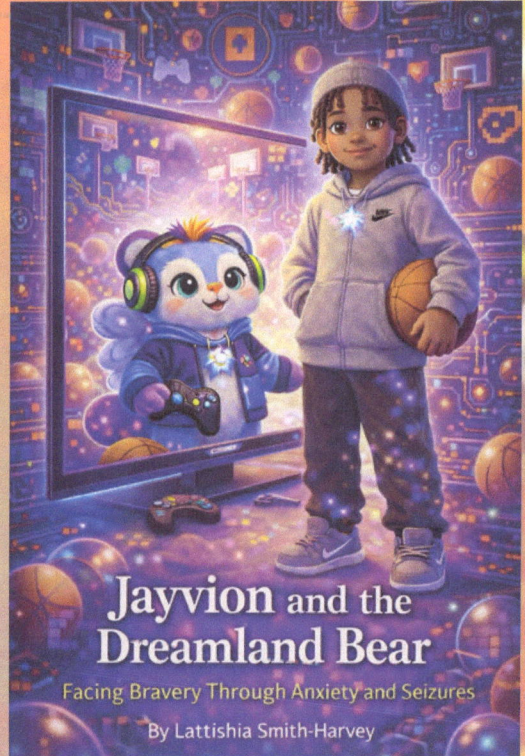

JAZELLE, HER ANGEL, AND HER DREAMLING

BY LATTISHIA SMITH HARVEY

When you lie down, you will not be afraid; your sleep will be sweet.
Proverbs 3:24

Jayvion and the Dreamland Bear

Facing Bravery Through Anxiety and Seizures

By Lattishia Smith-Harvey

AVAILABLE ON AMAZON

www.ingramcontent.com/pod-product-compliance
Lightning Source LLC
LaVergne TN
LVHW072122070426
835511LV00002B/63